Pain 2 Purpose

Shakila Kendall

Pain 2 Purpose

{ 1 }

From Pain to Purpose

(Series)
Author: Shakila Kendall
Cover Design: Shardell Martin
Self-Published
Copyright 2024 **by Shakila Kendall**

Pain to Purpose (Series)

Table Of Content

{ 3 }

Dedication

This book is dedicated to those who have been bleeding from their heart and are incapable of articulating their pain. God told me to write this series because He wanted you to know that you are not alone and that He sees you. There is always purpose in your pain, you must seek Him out to find what that purpose is. If you allow God into your situation, He will change it. Many times, we want God to come in the way we want but know that God has your best interest at heart so when He comes it will be the way you need!

Proverbs 19:21 *"Many are the plans in a person's heart, but it is the Lord's purpose that prevails"* **NIV**

Romans 8:28 *"And we know that all things work together for good to those who love God, to those who are the called according to His Purpose"* **NKJV**

"Shout out to pain because you took me to the dark and low place that I didn't think I could make it through, the confused place, the where are you Lord place, the I didn't see myself making it place. In these places it showed me the I didn't know me place, and it was the He kept me place and brought me through it all place and now I stand tall place but all of it would mean nothing if I didn't learn God's lesson that pain birth purpose and it birth's you to"-Shardell Martin

{ 4 }

Acknowledgements

Pain- Thank you for teaching me that I can overcome heartache, trauma and cycles of torment if I acknowledge and heal from pain.

Purpose-Thank you because in my darkest moments I was able to hold on to you.

Husband- Thank you for showing me that even when I cause others' pain that I am still worthy of love and that it is important to take accountability for the pain that we cause others.

Sister- Thank you because your unwavering support and tenacity to never give up is needed and appreciated.

Mom- Thank you for the motivational talks and supporting me through it all.

Pastor Leah- Thank you for allowing God to use you to light a fire in me to finish this book and for showing me that it's more than ok to be transparent about my struggles.

Pastor Chad- Thank you for always encouraging me to pursue and walk in purpose. You lead with such grace.

Reader- Thank you because all the pain I have experienced in this life, now allows me to help you through your pain.

God- Thank you, you are the real MVP and I cannot imagine a life without you in it!

{ 5 }

Beauty in Tragedy

S ometimes life can feel so tragic
      Almost like someone is doing magic against you
   To create your reality of calamity
   But thinking like that can cause insanity
   Next thing you know you're compromising your moral-
ity
   Time to create a new mentality
   Sometimes life can feel so tragic
   When you take hit after hit
   and you feel you don't deserve it one bit
   and it's hard to admit
   that sometimes the cause is the crimes
   That we commit
   and it's time to quit
   Those things that bring us so much pain
   Now don't go condemning yourself
   Awareness is crucial in order to seek help
   Sometimes life can feel so tragic
   Like you're drowning and there's no one to save you
   Like the path you're on was never paved for you

Almost like God never forgave you
For the sins of your past
And now He is repaying you with His wrath
Sometimes life can feel so tragic
That all you want to do is scream and cry
And ask God why?
Just know that He will answer you
So be prepared for the truth
Everything not black or white
Somethings are blue
Sometimes life can feel so tragic
Then you realize we have a bad habit
Of making things bigger than they are
Instead allow God to inhabit
your space
time to embrace the beauty in your tragedy
heal from the hurt and pain
let go of the gravity
fly above it all no more hitting walls
stand tall
sometimes life can feel so tragic
but there is an answer to it all
find the beauty in your tragedy!!!

{ 6 }

Accountability

Accountability is all about the fruit you produce
So no need to spruce
up the dirt
accountability makes us dig up the hurt
that we cause to ourselves and others
the seeds we planted
will determine the outcome of the fruit
ripe, bitter, sweet
the seeds we planted
will determine what we eat
fear, chaos, love, or peace
the soil has to be right for the seeds to grow
so how are you tending to this flow
called life?
cause you will reap what you sow
accountability equal responsibility
for the choices I make
not playing blame games for my mistakes
but relentlessly
examining ME and all the things I can't see

cause the blinders on my eyes causing me to tell lies
to me about me
when I want to hide
wearing a mask so I can only show the world parts of me
especially hiding parts that are ug-a-lee
time to own up to the choices we make
time to stop pretending and being fake
accountability is being owners of our choices
even when the consequences are bad
even when the results make us sad
your fruit can't grow if you're not honest about if you
watered it or not
the lying causes the production to stop
the good thing is it's never too late to turn it around
to start all over and till the ground
a fresh start is brewing
can't you feel the victories accruing
remember who you were created to be
a giant knows to take
accountability
so that they can truly be free!

Loss

Hurry hurry come quick
    My baby heart is asystole
Meaning it's no longer beating
God keep my baby soul
And I'm not sure if I'm only dreaming
God, I need you stat
Because now my line is going flat
I can't breathe
Because my baby loss their breathe
Lord show me how to live when a part of me just died
Teach me how to stay alive
During this indescribable loss
I want to be able to cross
Over not go under
There is always light in the thunder's roar
There is always purpose in an eagle's soar
I never felt a pain like this before
My rate is tachycardia
Heart beating so fast I don't know how long I'll last
Life right now is not a blast

Here comes the light at the end of the tunnel
This experience has made me humble
Many others around me suffered this fate
Never did I ever think it would land on my plate
Or show up at my gate
Now I've healed so my plane taking off
Or so I thought
Now I'll take a pause
***

Hurry hurry come quick
It's happening again this time blood everywhere
I know that's a lot to share
But I can no longer hide the truth
Of the trauma that this loss produced
Just when I thought I was moving on
Loss tried to pull me back in a whirlwind
Making me feel exposed to all my sin
Doc gave me the option to let it happen naturally
Or get another procedure
But this whole thing felt supernaturally
Like God was speaking and I didn't understand why
I froze like a silent seizure
As I lift my ears and head to the sky
Questioning wondering if I was the cause
Then doc said it's not your fault
It's like he could read my thoughts
Then I realize he was taught this line
I knew he didn't have the answers I needed
But on the inside, I was begging and pleading

I knew I couldn't put my body through that trauma again

Although my baby was gone, I was bothered by

Letting a device take the rest of my baby life

I screamed in agony no one to hold my hand but a stranger

In the moment all I felt was danger

So, no doc this time I'll let my body do it naturally

Although this is not naturally the way I intended it to go

I know God will heal me and He will continue to do so

There is always light in loss

There is always a reason and a cause

Only God can heal the grief

Only God can restore my belief!

Edited on 6/25/23

Now I'll take one last pause

Yup you guessed it

It happened again

But this time I won't be long cause now

I understand who gave me the strength

To endure and become so strong

I don't know why this keep

Happe-ning but I know I can help others through

What I went through time and time again!

*Although this poem is talking about my miscarriages, it was created to reflect the process of loss! Whether it be a loved one, miscarriage, traumatic event, marriage, or something/someone close to you. This "loss" is not just death. It can also be compared to losing yourself!

{ 8 }

Yesterday

Yesterday is the past
    yet somehow it effects last
letting go is easier said than done
when you can't pinpoint
where the pain begun
yesterday will never return
and still, it has such a strong hold
I reject this verdict it is adjourned
How can something no longer in existence
Be so persistent
in causing grief
The stronghold that yesterday has is beyond belief
But there is a way to be free
And it's not by letting go
But instead, you have to deal
With all the things you dread from your past
All the years you allowed the pain to last
You have to unpack and unravel
All the things you been through
Then call a verdict and hit the gavel

Decide whether you will allow the lies
of the enemy to preside
over your life or will you take back your power
and don't think twice
about it
yesterday is gone but you get to choose how to move on
healed or broken!

Toxicity

Poisonous, extremely harsh, malicious, harmful quality
        Words that define toxicity
    Yet we let it invade our domesticity
    Our bodies, our family our life
    Consuming us like an infection
    But we turn a blind eye to its detection
    Toxicity running rampant like a fever
    Temp so hot we thrive in it like beavers
    We have normalized this reality by not rising above
    Time to uproot this stigma from the way that we love
    Toxicity is like cancer to the bones
    So bitter and detrimental
    Keeps you from wanting to go home
    We toxic in our thoughts, behaviors, and our hearts
    But expect pure love from others
    Like our love don't reflect bark
    Bitter, spicy sometimes sweet
    Time to rip toxic love apart
    We are so finicky when it comes to our needs
    Yet we don't want to give

What we expect to receive
If you desire real love
Love yourself for real
No more consuming toxic chemicals
Through food, drugs, body fluids and scrubs
Learn to give yourself a hug
True love keeps no record of wrong and forgives
When you acknowledge and change your behavior
The fruit of your love will bloom
And infect those around you
Your time for pure love will come soon
Destroying generational curses
And creating safe spaces
For authenticity
And generational Blessings
No more 2nd guessing
if you can live in love, peace and harmony
time for a greater pressing
forward and leaving toxicity in the past
now let this be your last
time looking back
no more embracing any lack!

{ 10 }

Tranquility

(C alm)
    The storms of life are raging, boisterous and caging
    Yet we think it can be calmed by sagging
    This calm can only come from above
    This is real peace that is found in love
    In fact the greatest love
    When the python grips your neck
    And all you can do is hold your breath
    Your tears will speak words to heaven that you can't release
    Cause all you know is the pain run so deep
    You push pass the stronghold and release a cry
    That you didn't know you had
    That deep pain has now surfaced
    This is the perfect moment to turn to purpose
    We talk about "the calm before the storm"
    But there's a calm during the storm
    That allows your faith to form
    A Peace that surpasses your understanding

From a supernatural being that is demanding
His demands are what's best for our sake
They create a calm and help prevent mistakes
Real peace comes from knowing God
He will show you how to navigate the storm
And survive
Not only that but He will teach you to come alive
When you learn to be calm in the storm
You subdue the power that it had to form!

{ 11 }

Access Denied

Hey you, yeah you
    I remember the nights and times I cried
But this time your access is denied
Every struggle, pain and cycle were for a purpose
But I won't allow you to resurface
You tried to take me out
But your seeds of destruction caused me to sprout
At one point my heart was full of doubt
You tried to form those weapons against me
And you ain't know I was going to use your weapons to break free
Back then my portion was sorrow, heartache and demise
Now I feel alive
Trauma, cycles and pain you got to flee
You no longer have a stronghold over me
You can't live here no more
Now step on out the door
That I opened because my triggers bought so much emotion
Now say hello to the new me

The healed me

The whole me

Cause she is moving forward to the place I'm supposed
to be

Elevated in the spirit

With the one who created me

With life full of purpose

And life more abundantly

So past your access is denied from this point I intend to
thrive!

{ 12 }

Compassion

To have genuine concern for another's suffering
truly understanding the clustering
Of emotions that one can experience
When trauma has sent them in a state of delirium
We blame our parents for so much
Not realizing they blame their parents for so much
This is why our generations have been stuck
In cycles of unhealed trauma
Family functions producing drama after drama
Let's choose to unravel and unpack
Childhood wounds
So the family-dynamic can fulfill purpose and bloom
When thinking on the pain that family has caused
Consider their bleeding hearts
And childhood issues that were never resolved
It's not making excuses however it provides a reason
To why families have been broken in every season
Uncle, cousin or dad snuck into your room and touched
in places that were wrong

Aunt, sibling or mom snuck into your parent room in childhood

And they sung the same song

To their parent who didn't listen and the abuse continued

Now all they see is themselves in you

No one showed up for them

and they don't know how to come to your rescue

Their pain was unheard and now they lack compassion

Their innocence was stolen

And so was their ability to love properly

The pain they retained is now swollen

Or maybe your dad was so mean

Because his dad left him standing at the door screen

Or maybe your mom called you out of your name

Because her mom rejected her the same

Now we can see childhood trauma

Can have an everlasting effect if we don't unravel and unpack

Grandmas and grandpops aren't bitter just because

Some of them never had a real hug

Or heard a real I love you

And this cycle holds true

For some of us

We break this through the spirit of compassion

So that authentic love is everlasting

In our children

And in their children

Let's hold ourselves accountable

And stop cycles of trauma that seem insurmountable!

{ 13 }

Pain into Purpose

Now it's time to turn ALL this pain into purpose
Because God created me with purpose
In mind
I can't undo what's done but I can help
Others become
Who they were meant to be
By giving them a glimpse into me
And revealing they can be free
Event-ual-ly
If they allow God to deliver, heal and process
Them emot-ion-aly
One goal in life is to be whole
And you can't do that with a broken soul
So aht aht no more giving in
No more time to fold
Rise up King- Rise up Queen
I know you been hurting a long time
Now you can say you heard through the grapevine
That there's more to life than your pain
There's peace and happiness available

That you can sustain
It's in Christ Jesus
The name above all names
Don't let nobody tell you that's lame
I'm a living witness
Of the power that resides in Him
And now I know that same power resides in me
And that's how I became Free
Not temporarily but for eternity
Baby don't settle for momentary escape
When you can have a life of
Div-in-ity!

{ 14 }

Definitions

C alamity- grievous affliction; adversity; misery
    Condemn- to express an unfavorable or adverse judgment on; indicate strong disapproval of

Accountability-the state of being liable or answerable

Asystole- the absence of heartbeat; cardiac arrest

Agony- extreme and generally prolonged pain; intense physical or mental suffering.

Adjourned- formally ended or closed

Toxicity- the quality, relative degree, or specific degree of being toxic or poisonous

Detrimental- causing detriment, as loss or injury; damaging; harmful.

Tranquility- the quality or state of being tranquil; calmness; peacefulness; quiet; serenity

Demise- a person's death

Compassion- sympathetic pity and concern for the sufferings or misfortunes of others

Delirium- a disturbed state of mind or consciousness

Insurmountable- too great to be overcome

Divinity- divine nature (God like nature)